What Are

PROGRAMS AND APPLICATIONS?

Spotlight on Kids Can Code

Patricia Harris

PowerKiDS press
New York

Published in 2018 by The Rosen Publishing Group, Inc.
29 East 21st Street, New York, NY 10010

Copyright © 2018 by The Rosen Publishing Group, Inc.

All rights reserved. No part of this book may be reproduced in any form without permission in writing from the publisher, except by a reviewer.

First Edition

Editor: Elizabeth Krajnik
Book Design: Michael J. Flynn

Photo Credits: Cover Jetta Productions/David Atkinson/Getty Images; p. 5 doodle/Shutterstock.com; p. 7 Valentin Valkov/Shutterstock.com; p. 9 (Android) Gerisima/Shutterstock.com; p. 9 (iPhone) George Dolgikh/Shutterstock.com; pp. 11, 15 Dragon Images/Shutterstock.com; p. 13 Natee Meepian/ Shutterstock.com; p. 17 Chinnapong/Shutterstock.com; p. 21 carballo/Shutterstock.com.

Cataloging-in-Publication Data

Names: Harris, Patricia.
Title: What are programs and applications? / Patricia Harris.
Description: New York : PowerKids Press, 2018. | Series: Spotlight on kids can code | Includes index.
Identifiers: ISBN 9781508155249 (pbk.) | ISBN 9781508155126 (library bound) | ISBN 9781508154778 (6 pack)
Subjects: LCSH: Computer programming–Juvenile literature. | Application software–Juvenile literature. | Operating systems (Computers)–Juvenile literature.
Classification: LCC QA76.6 H37 2018 | DDC 005.1–dc23

Manufactured in the United States of America

CPSIA Compliance Information: Batch #BS17PK: For Further Information contact Rosen Publishing, New York, New York at 1-800-237-9932

Contents

What Are We Using?......................4

Applications Explained...................6

User Interface and Applications.......8

Apps vs. Programs.....................10

Device Drivers and GUIs..............12

Programming Software and
      Application Software..............14

"There's an App for That!"...........16

Creating Game Apps with Coding.......18

Text-Based Games.....................20

Understanding the Terms..............22

Glossary.............................23

Index................................24

Websites.............................24

What Are We Using?

Imagine having to write every line of code in a game while you're trying to play it. Do you want to swing a sword? If so, you'd better write the code quickly before a monster attacks! Would you like to go into a new room? If you're not playing in a game application, you'll need to program the room and the movements required to get there.

As computer users, we often don't think about the applications we use. We pick up our smartphone and go to a calendar application to check what's on our schedule for the day. We go to a weather application to help us decide whether we should wear a raincoat or a winter coat. We go to our laptop or tablet to write our English paper using a word processor.

This knight is about to fight a fire-breathing dragon. You might see a scene like this in a game application on your smartphone or tablet.

5

Applications Explained

Today, people often believe the term "application" and the term "program" mean the same thing. Both programs and applications are software. Software is a set of instructions for a computer, as opposed to **hardware**. Hardware doesn't work without software. Of course, new developments in hardware often call for new software. An application is a type of software that makes it possible for us to do a task. An application may consist of several parts working together to complete the task it is designed to do.

Applications haven't always been written for personal computers. Years ago, most people didn't have personal computers—only programmers used computers. Whenever a programmer wanted to complete a task on a computer, they used a programming language to write code, which told the computer what to do.

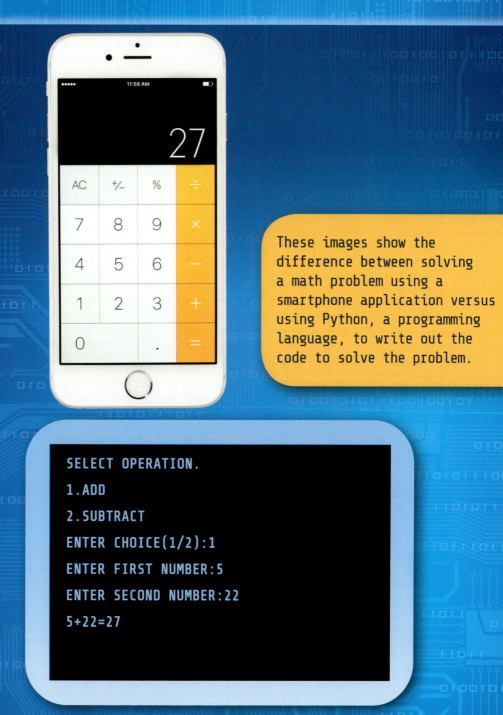

These images show the difference between solving a math problem using a smartphone application versus using Python, a programming language, to write out the code to solve the problem.

```
SELECT OPERATION.
1.ADD
2.SUBTRACT
ENTER CHOICE(1/2):1
ENTER FIRST NUMBER:5
ENTER SECOND NUMBER:22
5+22=27
```

User Interface and Applications

When people talk about an application, or app, they're usually referring to an app on a certain device, such as a smartphone or a tablet. Apps complete tasks with a certain user interface on a specific device. The user interface refers to the parts of a device with which a user interacts, such as a screen or a keyboard. A weather app, for example, gives the user information about the weather as it is at the time and over the next few days.

Certain apps only work on certain devices. For example, an iPhone app will only run on an iPhone. Apps for Android devices may look a lot like iPhone apps, but they were designed to work with the Android user interface. User interface designers keep all of these things in mind. They are the ones who design the elements that users see.

Breaking the Code

Shortening the term "application" to "app" has been popular for many years. Many people believe that this abbreviation came about when Apple launched the iPhone and the App Store. However, "app" has existed for a very long time—well before Apple created the iPhone. No one truly knows who began this trend.

Sometimes app developers copy apps to cheat the system. App developers copied the photo-editing app A Beautiful Mess to make money off Apple. One of the copycat apps was free, whereas the original is 99 cents.

Apps vs. Programs

Apps and computer programs aren't quite the same. Computer programs are often less **complex** than apps. A computer program is a set of instructions to be performed by the computer, such as code designed to test part of another program to see if it's working correctly. Programs may run on several devices and may not have a user interface. In this way, they are different from applications.

Programs can be understood from the point of view of software developers. Software developers are people who decide what software needs to do to meet the needs of users. They then write the code or tell others what code to write. If the software developers are designing applications rather than programs, they need to include a user interface and work with user interface designers.

Software developers work on the code that makes up a program.

11

Device Drivers and GUIs

There are three types of software. One type is system software. This type of software includes special programs such as device drivers, which make your computer's hardware work. System software also includes the operating system and the graphical user interface, or GUI, used to access the computer. A GUI is an interface through which a user interacts with an electronic device through icons and other **graphics**.

Today, we expect a GUI to be there when we turn our computer on, but this wasn't always the case. Years ago, people turned on their computers and had one command line on the screen. To access a program on their computer, they would have to write a command to tell that program to run. They couldn't just click on an icon on the computer's desktop. At that time, desktops and icons didn't exist yet.

Microsoft Disk Operating System, or MS-DOS, was a popular operating system in the 1980s and 1990s. It uses a command line interface. MS-DOS was replaced by GUIs and is infrequently used today.

Programming Software and Application Software

A second type of software is programming software. This is software that software developers and coders use to write programs using programming languages such as Pascal or C++. This software includes tools for editing and **debugging** software. There may also be links to use other programs inside your program, such as **compilers** and **interpreters**.

The third type of software is application software. There are many different types of application software. Internet browsers allow you to surf the web. Word processors and desktop publishing applications allow you to write text and put that text in many forms. **Databases** and spreadsheet applications allow you to work with numbers and organize information to make it easy to find and change.

The three types of software help us interact with computer **environments**. Without them, our relationship with computers would be much more difficult.

"There's an App for That!"

You can find apps to do just about anything you want. If you want to draw pictures on your smartphone, you can use a simple application called Sketches Pro. Sketches Pro is a good example of an application that was **modified** to work with new hardware. It can be used with a stylus, which is a pen-shaped device used with computers. The app can make the touch of a stylus **mimic** the brushstrokes of a paintbrush or other artists' tools.

If you want to touch up photos, you can use graphics applications to make many changes to your pictures. Adobe Photoshop is a graphics program for altering pictures. It can be purchased alone or as a package of programs—the Adobe Creative Cloud. This set of applications includes tools for video editing and more.

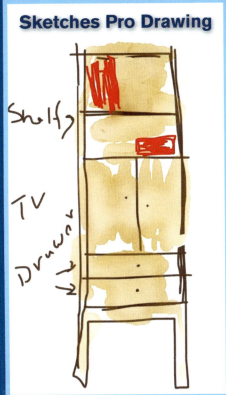

Sketches Pro Drawing

Applications must be developed or improved to work with new hardware. In 2010, Apple trademarked, or legally became the owner of, the phrase "There's an app for that" because the App Store had more apps than its competitors at that time.

Creating Game Apps with Coding

So what does it take to create a game app? It takes a lot of coding! Most users never see the code that goes into creating an app. The user might see a scene with a character that's doing something. Every time the scene changes, coding makes the change possible.

Before the programmers create the scene and the characters, they must think about what motions the characters will make as they move around in the scene. Then they code the character's actions.

Early computer games didn't include all the graphics you see in today's games. People played online text-based games. Instead of graphics showing a room, the room and the location of the characters and items in the room were described in the text of the game. Users moved around in the game by writing text commands.

> This game code is part of a program. It can run on any hardware that can run the programming language Python. It isn't an application, but it could become part of an application.

```python
1   #Function for combat
2    def Combat():
3      global game_state
4      player = game_state['players'][0]
5      enemy = game_state['npcs'][0]
6      global go
7      while go == True:
8          dmg = randint (0, player.strength)
9          edmg = randint (0, enemy.strength)
10         enemy.health -= dmg
11
12   if player.health <= 0:
13      os.system('cls')
14      print()
15      print("You have been slain by the enemy
        {}...".format(enemy.name))
16      go = False
17      leave = input("press enter to exit")
18
19    elif enemy.health <= 0:
20      os.system('cls')
21      print()
22      print("You hatve slain the enemy {}!".format(enemy.name))
23      go = False
24      leave = input("press any key to exit")
25
26    else:
27      os.system('cls')
28      with open("test.txt", "r") as in_·le:
29          text = in_·le.read()
30      print(text)
31      player.health -= edmg
32      print()
33      print("You attack the enemy {} for {} damage!"format(enemy.
        name, dmg))
34      print("The enemy has {} health left!".format(enemy...health))
```

Text-Based Games

The code for the text-based game on the previous page lets you see some of the **concepts** inside coding for game apps. The first line—"#Function for combat"—is a comment line that tells you that the code that follows is the code for combat. The following lines tell you that you need two characters:

```
player = game_state['players'][0]
enemy = game_state['npcs'][0]
```

These lines of code tell you that the hero has slain the enemy:

```
elif enemy.health <= 0:
os.system('cls')
print()
print("You have slain the enemy {}!".
format(enemy.name))
go = False
leave = input("press any key to exit")
```

Line one tells you that if the enemy's health is less than or equal to zero, the next lines of code should be followed. If the enemy's health is greater than zero, the rest of the code in this part is ignored.

20

In recent years, some gamers have returned to text-based games. These games are often referred to as interactive fiction. They used to be called text adventures.

Understanding the Terms

It's important to understand the difference between software, programs, and applications if you want to learn more about what you're doing when you use your computer or smartphone. For most users, these terms seem to have the same meaning. Today we can **download** apps to our computers, smartphones, and tablets!

Programs are the pieces of code that make a computer do specific tasks. Applications are programs or collections of programs that run on specific hardware and have a user interface. But programs aren't necessarily applications. Applications are designed for users—programs are not. The overall term for programs and applications is software, which makes the hardware work.

It's important for people who want to really understand the world of computers to know the small differences between these elements and how they all work together to help users complete tasks.

Glossary

compiler: A computer program or set of programs that changes the language in which a program was written into another computer language, such as binary code.

complex: Having many parts.

concept: A general idea.

database: A computerized system that makes it easy to search, select, and store information.

debug: To remove mistakes from a computer program.

download: To copy data from one computer to another, often over the Internet.

environment: The combination of computer hardware and software that allows a user to perform various tasks.

graphic: A picture or shape.

hardware: The physical parts of a computer such as a monitor or keyboard.

interpreter: A computer program that changes a high-level programming language into a lower-level programming language in order to follow its instructions.

mimic: To imitate very closely.

modify: To make changes to something.

Index

A
Adobe Creative Cloud, 16
Adobe Photoshop, 16
Android, 8
Apple, 8, 9, 17
application software, 14
App Store, 8, 17

C
C++, 14
code, 4, 6, 7, 10, 14, 18, 20, 22
compilers, 14

D
device drivers, 12

G
graphical user interface (GUI), 12, 13

H
hardware, 6, 12, 16, 17, 18, 22

I
interpreters, 14
iPhone, 8

L
laptop, 4

O
operating system, 12

P
Pascal, 14
programming language, 6, 7, 14, 18
programming software, 14
Python, 7, 18

S
Sketches Pro, 16
smartphone, 4, 7, 8, 16, 22
software, 6, 10, 12, 14, 15, 22
system software, 12

T
tablet, 4, 8, 22
text-based games, 18, 20, 21

U
user interface, 8, 10, 22

Websites

Due to the changing nature of Internet links, PowerKids Press has developed an online list of websites related to the subject of this book. This site is updated regularly. Please use this link to access the list: www.powerkidslinks.com/skcc/progapp